UP CLOSE WITH
SPIDERS

Alexandra Siy and Dennis Kunkel

Holiday House / New York

To Rory, some son—terrific, radiant, and humble
Love, Spidermom—A. S.

To Chris Porter, with deep gratitude for your colorizations of my electron micrographs, which come alive with your precision masking and vivid colors. A special thank-you to my mother, who is always willing to collect bugs and spiders for her son!—D. K.

ACKNOWLEDGMENTS
We are grateful to all the people who helped us create this book: the students at the Shining Mountain Waldorf School in Boulder, Colorado, especially Rebecca Anne Blum and Devon Wycoff, who collected arachnids for Dennis to image; Lynette Schimming, who created the spider eye patterns; and the scientists who provided information, spider identifications and outstanding images for the book: Rod Crawford, Burke Museum, Seattle; Dr. David Penney, Honorary Lecturer, Faculty of Life Sciences (Preziosi Lab), University of Manchester, UK; Dr. Stefan K. Hetz, Humboldt-Universität zu Berlin, Germany; Robert B. Suter, PhD, Editor-in-Chief, *Journal of Arachnology;* Charles E. Griswold, PhD, Schlinger Curator of Arachnology (Emeritus), Department of Entomology, California Academy of Sciences and the John Guy Vassar Professor of Biology, Emeritus, Vassar College; Paula E. Cushing, PhD, Curator of Invertebrate Zoology, Denver Museum of Nature and Science; Dr. Mark S. Harvey, Senior Curator and Head, Department of Terrestrial Zoology, Western Australian Museum; Darrell Ubick of the California Academy of Sciences; Lou Sorkin, Senior Scientific Assistant, American Museum of Natural History; Dr. Norman I. Platnick, Senior Scientist and Peter J. Solomon Family Curator Emeritus of Spiders, Division of Invertebrate Zoology, American Museum of Natural History; Gordon Smith, Pacific Islands Fish and Wildlife Office, Honolulu, HI. Also special thanks to Chris Porter for her excellent colorizations and the Siy kids, who have promised to "like" spiders from now on. Special thanks to our ever-patient and brilliant editor, Mary Cash, whose love of spiders made this book possible, and art director Claire Counihan, who helped bring our vision to life.

HOLIDAY HOUSE is registered in the U.S. Patent and Trademark Office.
Printed and Bound in August 2018 at Tien Wah Press, Johor Bahru, Johor, Malaysia.
www.holidayhouse.com
3 5 7 9 10 8 6 4 2

Originally published in hardcover as *Spidermania: Friends on the Web.*
The Library of Congress has cataloged the prior edition as follows:
Library of Congress Cataloging-in-Publication Data
Siy, Alexandra, author.
Spidermania : friends on the web / by Alexandra Siy and [photomicrographs by] Dennis Kunkel. — First edition.
pages cm
Audience: Ages 6-10.
Audience: Grades 4-6.
Includes bibliographical references and index.
ISBN 978-0-8234-2871-7 (hardcover)
1. Spiders—Juvenile literature. I. Kunkel, Dennis, author, illustrator. II. Title.
QL458.4.S594 2015
595.4'4—dc23
2014017139
ISBN 978-0-8234-4044-3 (paperback)

The brightly colored, magnified images of arachnids were made with a high-power scanning electron microscope (SEM) and are referred to as electron micrographs (EM). Other pictures were taken with a camera and are labeled as photographs. Captions of EM images include how many times the image is magnified from the original size of the specimen using the symbol "x."

CONTENTS

Spiderweb in Sabine
National Wildlife Refuge
in Louisiana.

This lucky-to-be-alive crab spider was captured by a photographer's camera in Germany for the world to admire.

A Short, Funny Video

It's springtime in New Jersey, and a group of fourth graders are visiting Governor Chris Christie. The governor loves kids (he has four of his own), and regularly hosts students in his office, where he answers their questions about government, current events and other interesting things. But during this visit, there's something much smaller than a ten-year-old that has caught his attention. The class crowds around his desk, trying to see it.

The governor bends over to get a closer look.

"Where is he?" he asks. "Ah, there he is."

"Let's staple it!" shouts a boy.

But before anyone can reach for the stapler, or any other piece of lethal office equipment—down comes the governor's hand.

Bam! Splat!

Children cheer, some clap. A few laugh. Life goes on. Except, of course, for the spider.

The governor tweets: *Earlier today I saved a few school children from a spider.*

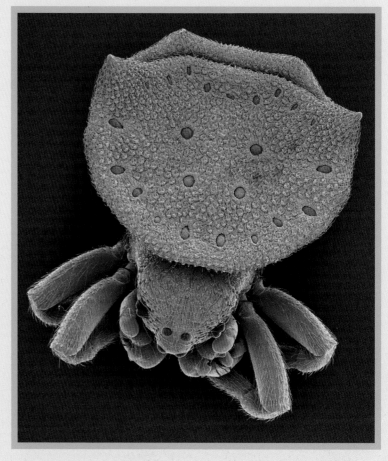

The spiny-backed orb-weaver is shown 20 times (x20) larger than its actual size. It has a hard, flat body with three pairs of spines projecting from the edge of its abdomen. It catches insects in its vertical orb web.

Then he posts a video on YouTube called "Governor Christie Saves School Children From Spider." It's a short, funny video, unless you are a spider . . . or a friend of one.

Most people don't like spiders. Many are afraid of them. "Arachnophobia" is the scientific term for fear of spiders.

Spiders, scorpions, ticks and mites are types of arachnids—all adult arachnids have four pairs of jointed legs. But only spiders have spinnerets: the parts that make silk.

Action Figures

A spider has two distinct body parts. The front part, called the prosoma, is sandwiched between two plates of armor. The top plate is called the carapace, and the bottom plate is the sternum. Sticking out from between the plates of armor are four pairs of walking legs, a pair of pincer-like mouthparts called chelicerae (chell-is-er-ay) and two pedipalps, or "foot feelers." These appendages are all about action—running, jumping, climbing, grabbing, digging, biting, building and chewing.

The back part is a soft, expandable sack called the abdomen. The churning gut, beating heart, breathing book lungs (spider lungs look like stacks of pages in a book), egg- or sperm-producing organs and silk-making glands are hidden inside.

The underside of a black widow showing important structures from top to bottom: eyes (purple), chelicerae (pink), fangs (orange), sternum (yellow), abdomen (olive green) and spinnerets (teal). (x24)

Class Arachnida

Scorpions
Order: *Scorpionida*

Spiders
Order: *Araneae*

Ticks
Order: *Acari*

Scorpions, spiders and ticks all have four pairs of legs and are classified as arachnids. The illustration does not show relative size or scale.

Stronger than Steel

But the most spectacular action of the spider, indeed, one of the most amazing achievements of any animal on Earth, is the creation and use of silk. The seven varieties of spider silk can be stronger than steel, tougher than nylon, stretchier than a bungee cord and stickier than glue.

Silk is a liquid protein, similar to milk, and is formed by glands inside the spider's abdomen. Tiny tubes transport the liquid silk to spigots located on the spinnerets. As the liquid is forced out of the spigots and pulled by the spider, it is transformed into a solid thread.

Pound for pound, silk is stronger than steel. But unlike steel, its stretchiness prevents it from breaking under stress. The dragline is the super-strong thread that trails behind the spider, ready to drop it to safety. The silk that encloses an egg case is waterproof and tough—about three times as sturdy as Kevlar (a man-made material used to make bulletproof vests, cut-proof gloves and super-light kayaks).

Inside the egg case, the silk is soft and fluffy. There's also special silk for wrapping eggs and several kinds for building webs.

7

EM of black widow spinnerets. A silk thread (green) is seen coming out of one of the three pairs of spinnerets (shown in yellow, orange, brown) located on the tip of the spider's abdomen. (x162)

EM of the nozzle-shaped spigots (green), which are located on the spinnerets and release silk (peach color) from their tips. The strong muscles that move the spinnerets also force liquid silk through the narrow spigots. This pressure, as well as the pulling action by the spider, changes the liquid silk into a solid, flexible thread. (x1,485)

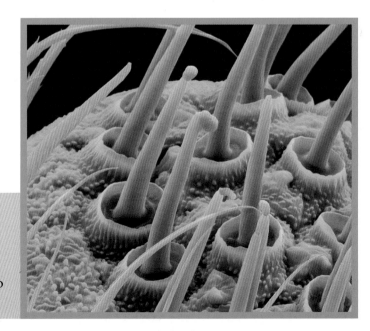

Silk is strong, tough, flexible, lightweight, waterproof, anti-germ, hypoallergenic (doesn't cause allergic reactions) and totally biodegradable. Spider silk has been used to bandage wounds because of its anti-germ and hypoallergenic properties. Silk is inspiring inventors to design new high-performance fibers that are helpful to humans and don't pollute the environment. Silk alone should be reason enough for everyone to absolutely adore spiders! But many of us don't. . . .

A cobweb weaver has three claws (orange), including a smooth middle claw used for grasping silk threads while weaving a web. All spiders have two or three claws located at the tips of their legs. (x1,215)

EM of silk strands spun by a black widow spider for an egg case. Notice how thick strands branch into several thinner strands. This type of silk is called multi-stranded. (x1,500)

Twin Fangs

Perhaps it's the twin fangs that trigger fear. Located at the tips of the chelicerae, spider fangs inject venom into prey, causing loss of movement (paralysis) and sometimes death. Birds avoid eating certain spiders because their venom can cause sickness. Bright markings, such as the red hourglass on the black widow, are a warning to hungry predators: "Beware! I taste bad! I will make you sick!"

But not all spiders have such bold markings that give away their identity. To know a spider you must first look into its eyes.

A female black widow spider (*Latrodectus mactans*) spins her web on a tree branch. The characteristic red hourglass design on the underside of the abdomen can also be yellow, orange or white.

This photograph of an endangered Kaua'i cave wolf spider, taken by a scientist inside a narrow tunnel known as a lava tube, shows baby spiders (spiderlings) attached to their mother's back. Spikes on their legs connect with the hooks on the mother's branch-like "hairs." The adult spider is about ½ inch (1.3 cm) long. The shiny black structures are the chelicerae.

Family Eyes

There are 114 spider families. They are sometimes identified by the arrangement of their eyes. Ninety-nine percent of spider families have eight eyes, but some have six, four, two or none.

Some cave dwellers, such as the Hawaiian Kaua'i cave wolf spider, called the *pe'e pe'e maka 'ole*, or the "no-eyed, big-eyed wolf spider," have no eyes at all. How can a spider be no-eyed and big-eyed at the same time? The Kaua'i cave spider belongs to the wolf spider family, commonly called "big-eyed" spiders because most members of this group have two big front eyes. Since this species lives in the dark and doesn't need eyes, it is also called "no-eyed."

This image shows the distinctive eye pattern of a spider from the Sicariidae family, commonly called recluse spiders. Look on page 42 for more images of spider eye patterns.

The brown recluse is a smallish (11 mm) and fragile spider that delivers a poisonous bite if disturbed from its hiding place, sometimes under a towel or inside a shoe. Note its six eyes (green) and its two fangs (orange). Toxic venom is delivered through an opening near the end of each fang, similar to the opening in a hypodermic needle. (x35)

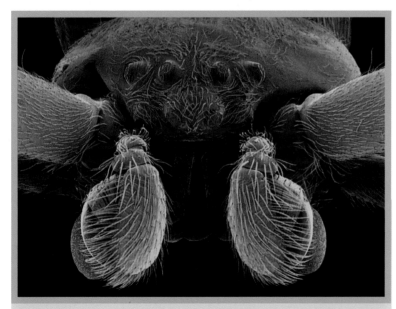

This EM of a garden spider shows its two rows of eyes (purple), all of which are the same size. (x83)

Some spider families consist of just one species. Others include dozens, hundreds or even thousands of different species. The jumping-spider family has the most—more than 5,600!

The *World Spider Catalog* lists the names of all the spider families and updates the inventory often with newly discovered species. On average, a new species is discovered every day. Scientists estimate there are at least 100,000 different spider species living on Earth today.

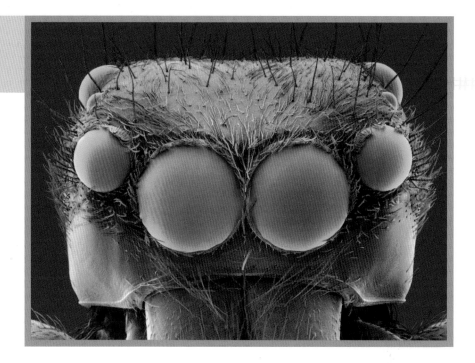

This image of a jumping spider shows its distinctive eye pattern (green), which makes it easy to identify. (x43)

Living Fossils

Spiders have lived on Earth a lot longer than humans. About 415 million years ago, arachnids were among the first animals to walk the earth. The first spiders appeared on the planet around 390 million years ago.

Some types of spiders haven't changed much from their ancient ancestors. These "living fossils" are known as the Mygalomorphae, or "primitive," spiders. Mygalomorphs, such as tarantulas, trap-door spiders and funnel-web spiders, are large and hairy and live mostly underground.

One characteristic of the primitive spider is its fangs that stab down like a pair of chopsticks. It has powerful chelicerae, but cannot grasp and pick up prey because its jaws cannot move from side to side. Instead, the spider drags its victim while holding it against the ground.

The Goliath birdeater tarantula is a primitive spider that measures one foot across and has one-inch-long fangs. There are at least 950 species of tarantulas, which are not only the biggest, but also the longest-lived, spiders. Males can live a dozen years, females at least twice that long.

This is a photograph of a fossilized spider in 16-million-year-old Dominican amber. It is from the family of mesh-web weavers (*Dictynidae*).

A head-on photo of a female Brazilian salmon pink birdeater tarantula shows its leg span of 10 inches, which makes it the third-largest spider species on Earth.

Primitive spiders have one or two silk glands that make silk needed for a life lived on and under the ground. A trap-door spider, for example, spins silk to line its underground burrow. Some trap-door spiders (but not all) make a sneaky silk hatch to a trap that catches unsuspecting prey as it walks, crawls, slithers or slides atop their lairs.

A spider can sense minuscule movements of silk with super-sensitive body and leg setae, some of which look like hairs. Even the slightest vibration signals the spider to leap out of hiding and ambush its victim.

The burrow of a funnel-web spider has a silken entrance hall leading into a narrow tunnel. At night, the spider sits inside this doorway with its front legs touching the silk trip lines it has rigged across the forest floor. Like a patient fisherman, the spider sits still until a cockroach, beetle or lizard trips on its line. When it senses a vibration, it pounces. Then it bites the prey and wraps it in silk.

Bite-Size Bites

The ingredients in spider venom can kill or paralyze prey, usually insects, small animals or other spiders, rather than people.

Tarantulas are the subjects of great fear, but they have weak venom. In fact, bee stings can be far more deadly than most spider bites.

Australian funnel-web spiders are world famous for their toxic venom, but they rarely bite people, and then only in self-defense when they are alarmed or threatened. The last time a human died from the bite of an Australian funnel-web spider was in 1979, the year before the lifesaving antivenom was available. Another Australian spider called the redback is also known for its deadly bite. But unlike the large, primitive funnel-web spider, the redback is classified as an araneomorph, or "modern," spider.

The Web Masters

At least 90 percent of all spiders are modern—the name of their scientific group, Araneomorphae, means "true spiders." Modern spiders evolved over millions of years, and as they changed, new forms of silk developed, allowing them to elevate themselves to the "high life." Using silk as draglines and for building webs above the ground, modern spiders were the first web masters, about 310 million years ahead of the geeky guys who thought up the Internet!

Scientists have identified more than forty-six thousand species of spiders (both primitive and modern) worldwide. Living in all kinds of environments, including mountaintops, deserts, caves and seashores, spiders have adapted to their surroundings in amazing ways.

Maybe if we got to know spiders, we wouldn't react with screams and smacks. Maybe we could even become friends.

The diving bell spider lives underwater, but comes to the surface once a day for air. (x82)

Diving Bell Spider

A diving bell spider attached to an air bubble beneath its underwater web.

The diving bell spider is the only known spider in the world that lives its entire life underwater. It is a web weaver, constructing an underwater web threaded to a water plant. But this web is for trapping air, not prey.

The diving bell spider climbs up a plant to reach the water's surface, where it floats on its back. Hairs on its body trap air, forming a bubble around the spider. Air enters slits in its abdomen and flows into book lungs, which are made from a stack of thin membranes that look like miniature pages in a book. Blue-colored blood flowing around the membranes picks up oxygen and carries it throughout the spider's body. Spider blood is blue because it contains the element copper rather than iron, the element that makes human blood red.

When the spider crawls along underwater plants back down to its web, its hairy legs sweep the air bubbles under the sheet of silk, inflating it like a balloon. The bubbles of air shimmer underwater like a silver coat; for this reason the scientific name of the diving bell spider is *Argyroneta aquatica*, Latin for "silvery net in the water."

Diving bell spiders have feathery hairs on their bodies that trap air bubbles at the surface of the water. These structures grow out of slipper-shaped holes in the exoskeleton. (x945)

Diving bell spiders capture insects, small fish and other small water creatures. Then they carry them into their underwater air chambers in which they eat, mate and lay eggs inside an egg sac. A few days after hatching, the spiderlings swim away and build diving bells of their own. If all that isn't amazing enough, the underwater web also works like a gill. It can take oxygen directly out of the surrounding water.

Diving bell spiders are found in ponds and slow-moving streams in Europe and northern Asia. People fascinated by the diving bell spiders' unique lifestyle capture and remove them from their natural habitat, a practice that could endanger their survival.

Fishing Spider

Although the diving bell spider is the only spider that lives underwater, there are many spider species that live on it.

On a dark, speckled rock, the white-banded fishing spider looks dark and speckled. Move it to a sun-bleached dock, and its color lightens to match the gray wood. Place it on moss, and its abdomen turns green. Blending in comes in handy for fishing spiders, those big, hairy hunters hiding on the banks of ponds, lakes and slow-moving streams.

This is an EM image of a young white-banded fishing spider (*Dolomedes albineus*) measuring about ¾ inch in size. It shows the chelicerae (pink), fangs (orange), eyes (yellow) and palps (blue). (x4.2)

WALKING ON WATER

A fishing spider (*Dolomedes tenebrosus*) rests on a dock in South Carolina.

Despite their large size, fishing spiders are light enough to walk on water. The hairs on the bottoms of their legs create a larger area over which to spread their weight. This helps keep them afloat. Some fishing spiders are more than one inch (30 mm) long. They're the ones people spot hanging out on the dock and scaring everyone into the water.

Sometimes a fishing spider lures a small fish to the surface by placing its leg in the water. If a little fish comes near, the spider dives in and grabs it. If a big fish appears, the spider jumps out of reach. It is easier for a spider to catch insects than for it to capture fish and tadpoles. While hunting insects, the spider moves across the water by rowing its second and third pairs of legs like oars. Sensitive hairs and other receptors on its legs detect tiny ripples on the water made by floating insects. Even a slight vibration signals the spider to pounce. Then the fishing spider drags its prey ashore to eat.

An EM of the fishing spider leg shows its setae (yellow) and other small sensory "hairs" (blue, green, orange). (x66)

NURSERY WEBS

Fishing spiders belong to the family called nursery-web spiders. Spiderlings are held inside a giant, round sac secured to their mother's spinnerets and gripped by her jaw-like chelicerae. The mother spider looks like she's holding on to a fuzzy yellow exercise ball. When the eggs are ready to hatch, she places the sac on a leaf and spins a web around it. Then she slashes it open and her spiderlings tumble into the nursery web, where she guards them until their first molt.

This EM of a female daddy longlegs spider (*Physocyclus mexicanus*) shows her slender palps (blue), chelicerae (teal), eyes (red) and fangs (pink). (x4.8)

Daddy Longlegs Spider

The fishing spider's name is just right. But how about the daddy longlegs spider? Its name is confusing. True, daddy longlegs spiders have long legs, but not all are daddies. In fact, the daddy longlegs spider in the picture might have been a mommy. And it was definitely a female.

You can tell the sex of a spider by looking at its pedipalps (or palps for short). These are the short pair of limbs between the first set of legs and the chelicerae. The word pedipalp means "foot feeler," but it's actually a mouthpart used for handling prey.

Female palps, like this girl's, taper to a stylish tip. But a sexually mature male's palps are larger and fuller, looking a bit like miniature boxing gloves. It is very difficult, if not impossible, to determine the sex of a young spider when its palps are still underdeveloped.

Females spin a few strands of silk to tie together their eggs. They carry them in their mouths. Daddy longlegs spiders have either six or eight closely spaced eyes, and weave tangled webs that snare prey. When threatened, they vibrate in their webs to scare away the intruder.

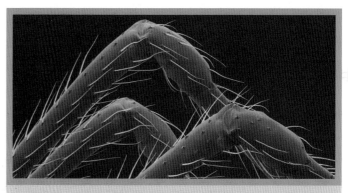

EM of a daddy longlegs spider's legs showing the patellas, or knee joints. All spiders have jointed legs consisting of seven sections, or segments. Hair-like structures called setae sense the environment. (x74)

SPIDER MYTH

Don't confuse daddy longlegs spiders with the well-known arachnids called daddy longlegs. These aren't even spiders, but harvestmen. They have two eyes and pill-shaped bodies. They can't make silk, and most don't have fangs. Those with fangs have no venom.

Wouldn't it be less confusing if daddy longlegs spiders went by a different name? Well, they do. Some are also called cellar spiders because they're found in basements and other dark places such as garages, caves and under dead leaves.

Many people say, "Daddy longlegs are one of the most poisonous spiders, but their fangs are too short to bite humans."

This is a myth, meaning it's totally not true! There is no record of a human ever being harmed by the bite of a daddy longlegs spider. And there is no scientific evidence suggesting its venom is more poisonous than any other spider venom.

This photo of a harvestman shows its pill-shaped body. It doesn't have fangs or venom. Harvestmen are arachnids because they have eight legs, but they are not spiders.

Wolf Spider

Most spiders are either hunters or web builders. Web builders snare their prey in cobwebs, sheet webs, funnel webs and orb webs. Hunters catch their prey using their legs, pedipalps and chelicerae with fangs.

The wolf spider, as its name suggests, is primarily a hunter. Some wolf spiders also build webs. Depending on the species, wolf spiders can be nocturnal (active at night) or diurnal (active in the daytime). They are found all over the world, even in the Arctic and on high mountains. Unlike wolves, wolf spiders hunt alone, not in packs. Some are wandering hobos—seeking, stalking and assailing prey on the ground. Some are sedentary shut-ins—sitting, waiting and ambushing prey from their miniature forts or large sheet webs.

A wolf spider detects the vibrations of a mosquito's beating wings, or a grasshopper's footsteps, with the sensitive setae (hairs) and other tiny receptors that cover its body. Its big eyes are just good enough to see an insect when it comes close enough to snatch.

This EM of a wolf spider (*Hogna carolinensis*) shows its distinctive eye pattern: four small eyes in a row and two very large eyes above, with another pair on either side of the head (shown in purple). Its palps are shown in green and its chelicerae in orange. (x4.6)

The feathery hairs (orange) on the wolf spider's abdomen are super-sensitive to vibrations, including sound waves. Hooked bristles (yellow) help spiderlings hold on tight. (x790)

When a wolf spider moves, it runs—over stones, across the grass, up a plant stem. Its leg movement is controlled by blood pressure. By increasing or decreasing its heart rate, the

A wolf spider (*Hogna helluo*) on the prowl.

spider can control the extension of its legs. The spider uses its muscles to control the flexing motion of its legs. Spiders have "four-leg drive": their legs move up and down, so four legs (two on each side) are touching the ground when the other four legs are in the air.

A mother wolf spider runs with her pea-size egg sac hanging from the spinnerets on her abdomen. After the spiderlings hatch, they ride along on the back of their mother's abdomen by clinging to her hook-like bristles.

Black Widow

Black widows belong to the group of spiders called cobweb weavers. Venom from a female black widow is toxic to humans and causes extreme muscle pain. But the bite is rarely fatal, because treatment with antivenom is highly effective.

The female spins her ultra-strong web, then hangs from it upside down while waiting for a visit from her "boyfriend."

A widow is a woman whose husband has died. The female black widow spider is often accused of eating the male either during or after mating with him. Usually, the male black widow (which weighs about 5 mg) mates with a super-size female (at about 100 mg) . . . then runs away.

The large palps (purple) identify this black widow spider (*Latrodectus variolus*) as a male. (x4.7)

23

This EM close-up of a male black widow shows large palps (light green) extending between the first pair of legs and the chelicerae (pink). During mating, the long coiled ducts (orange) are stretched out and placed into two openings in the female's abdomen. (x38)

FLIRTY DANCING

But the black widow has a cousin that does devour her mate. The female Australian redback spider eats him—unless he dances for at least one hundred minutes. Usually the male cuts short his dance in order to mate sooner. During the process he twists and somersaults, piercing his abdomen on the female's fangs. But he lives long enough to mate.

All animals that reproduce sexually make eggs and sperm. The purpose of mating is to unite an egg cell from the mother with a sperm cell from the father. Together the egg and sperm create a brand-new living being.

Male spiders of many species, including the black widow and Australian redback, spin a small sheet of silk called a sperm web. The male presses his body against the edge of the sperm web until a droplet containing sperm squirts out of an opening in his abdomen and drips onto the web. He fills his palps with sperm by dipping them into the droplet. Then he goes courting.

Each spider species has a different style of courtship depending on its vision and ability to see and detect sounds, smells and vibrations. Males may wave their palps and legs, bang their palps on the ground, vibrate their abdomens, deliver a silk-wrapped gift of a fly or do a dance. Some females give off alluring chemical smells called pheromones (which act like sexy perfume) to attract males. Female black widows are attracted to chemicals given off by the male's silk.

Successful courtship leads to mating. Some spiders get together while hanging from a web in an upside-down hug. Others remain on the ground and stay as far apart from each other as possible, depending on how far the male's palps can reach. But in every case sperm is transferred from ducts in the male's palps into an opening in the female's abdomen.

The female stores the sperm in her body until she is ready to lay eggs. An egg is fertilized when it unites with one sperm immediately before the egg is laid. Most spiders lay hundreds or even thousands of eggs in a few minutes. But a few teensy-weensy spiders lay only one—or in the case of *Oonops*, a genus of small spiders about the length of an average exclamation point, two!

This egg from a black widow spider (*Latrodectus hesperus*) measures about 1 mm. Hundreds of eggs develop inside a marble-size silk sac attached to the widow's web. (x77)

Sac Spider

The adult male sac spider chooses an immature female to be his future mate. Then he protects her as she grows into an adult.

As a spider grows in size, it must molt to shed its too-tight outer shell, or exoskeleton. Spiders molt between five and ten times, depending on their final adult size—a small sac spider molts fewer times than a large tarantula.

In preparation for molting, the sac spider stops eating and goes into hiding. When it's ready to molt, it suspends itself upside down from a silk thread. Its heart beats faster and faster, pumping fluid up into the prosoma. This increases the pressure inside the body and causes the exoskeleton to split down each side. Then

This EM of an adult female sac spider (*Anyphaena dixiana*) shows off its distinct eye pattern (red). The two eyes in back are reflective, an adaptation that helps the spider see in the dark. Also called leaf-curling sac spiders, members of this family are solitary nocturnal hunters, hiding alone in their silken bedrooms during the day and wandering around all night in search of prey. (x91)

the spider pulls its limbs out of its old skin. Sometimes a leg gets stuck and the spider dies. Usually the spider hangs from a thread suspended from its old skeleton until its new one hardens and its legs are sturdy enough for walking.

COFFIN AND CRIB

Soon after the female sac spider's final molt, while her new exoskeleton is still soft, she mates with the male that has stayed close by her for most of her life. A few weeks later, she builds a tiny bedroom by folding a blade of grass into a cone-shaped pod. She crawls into her room, lays her eggs inside a sac and seals herself in with sticky silk. Then she dies. After the spiderlings hatch, they feast on their mother's body until they are old enough to live on their own.

When the hatchlings are ready to leave their grass pod, they go ballooning. Spiderlings of many species are carried on the wind like tiny kites attached to silk strings.

A spiderling launches itself by releasing ultra-light silk, called gossamer, from its spinnerets while standing on tiptoes with its rear end pointed toward the sky. Winds or air currents carry it away. The distance the spider travels depends on its size and the weather. Ballooning spiders have traveled into the upper atmosphere and even across oceans.

This sac spider hatchling (also known as a spiderling) is in an early stage of development, before the eyes have appeared. Its spinnerets (gray), located on the tip of its abdomen, lack spigots, the tiny nozzles that extrude silk. (x69)

Jumping Spider

A dragline is a safety harness that prevents a spider from crashing to the ground. If a jumping spider misses its mark, it uses its two pairs of front legs to climb up its dragline to its starting place. The old dragline doesn't go to waste but is recycled into a snack. The spider uses its palps to stuff the high-protein treat into its mouth as it climbs. The dragline also works like a brake. By controlling how much dragline silk it releases, the spider can slow itself down as it flies toward its target.

This EM of a jumping spider (*Plexippus paykulli*) shows its hairy pedipalps (pink), which the spider uses like a cleaning brush to wipe off its two large "main eyes," located in the center of its head. The main eyes are capable of forming a detailed image. (x15)

If humans were as athletic as jumping spiders, the world record for the long jump would be more than one hundred feet, instead of less than thirty. Jumping spiders got their name because the male often jumps away from the female during his complicated courtship, which includes dancing, palp drumming, leg waving and showing off his stylish colors. Detecting these behaviors requires excellent vision.

BIONIC EYES

Spiders detect movements, vibrations and chemical tastes with highly sensitive body hairs and other microscopic receptors. Most spiders can see movement and light, but don't see a focused image. Jumping spiders are among the few that do.

The jumping spider's body is covered with leaf-like scales (yellow), which surround sensory hairs (blue) used for detecting movement and sounds. The scales either reflect light and appear white, or shimmer with rainbow colors due to diffraction of light. (x895)

Jumping spiders not only have the best sight, they are regarded as the world's best-looking spiders. Their fabulous furry bodies may sport zebra-ish stripes, leopard-like spots, chic colors, designer legs, shimmering scales and metallic-green chelicerae, depending on the species. Still, some jumping spiders look drab—with at least 5,678 jumping-spider species, some are bound to be dreary, dowdy or downright dull.

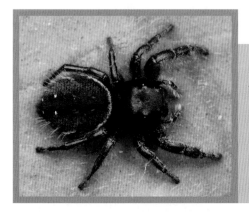

This photograph of an adult female redback jumping spider (*Phidippus johnsoni*) was shot in California. This spider is very common throughout North America. It is *not* related to the venomous Australian redback spider and is sometimes called the Johnson Jumper to avoid confusion. It grows to be about ¾ inch (1.9 cm) in length.

Unlike the sac spider, which slinks around mainly at night, the jumping spider hunts in the daytime. A sun worshipper, it can see as well as most humans.

Jumping spiders have two main eyes that work something like a camera lens. By focusing in on an insect, while at the same time blurring out objects in the distance, the jumping spider can determine how far it needs to leap. Jumping spiders are the only animals known to have this superpower.

The jumping spider has eight eyes (blue) that allow it to see in an almost 180° arc without having to move its head. The two large eyes in front are called the anterior middle eyes and are the "main eyes," which can form an image. The "secondary eyes" are located on the sides (lateral eyes) and in the back (posterior eyes), and detect motion. (x72)

Another member of the jumping-spider family holds a different kind of world record. It's the only non-carnivorous spider known. Named *Bagheera kiplingi*, after Bagheera, the panther in *The Jungle Book* by Rudyard Kipling, this spider lives in Central America and eats the buds of the acacia plant, although it has also been known to snack on ant larvae.

Crab Spider

Crab spiders are also called flower spiders because they often match the pink, yellow or green color of the flowers or leaves on which they wait. Some species can change their color to match different backgrounds. A few are white and look a lot like a splotch of bird poop.

This crab spider (*Misumena vatia*) appears to be meditating in a difficult yoga pose! In nature the camouflaged crab spider sits completely still with its long legs outstretched, waiting to grab a passing insect. In this image the palps are yellow, the fangs are orange and the chelicerae are colored brown. (x17)

A petite hunter, the crab spider's tactic is to lie in wait (see photo on page 4). Its small eyes can see insects clearly at close range and detect movements from a distance of about eight inches.

Despite their large size, bees and butterflies feeding on flower nectar and pollen can fall prey. The crab spider has long front legs that reach out and grab insects. Then its fangs paralyze the victim with a dose of potent poison.

Some spiders can chew their prey, crushing it into smaller pieces with tiny "teeth." But the crab spider has hairs instead of teeth on its chelicerae—it cannot chew its food at all. Crab spiders, and indeed all spiders, digest their prey into high-energy, high-protein smoothies.

Powerful stomach juices squirted into the insect's body through spider bite holes dissolve the prey's organs and flesh into liquid. Then the spider sucks in the nutritious drink by flexing its strong stomach. Bristles located around the spider's mouth strain out any solid particles.

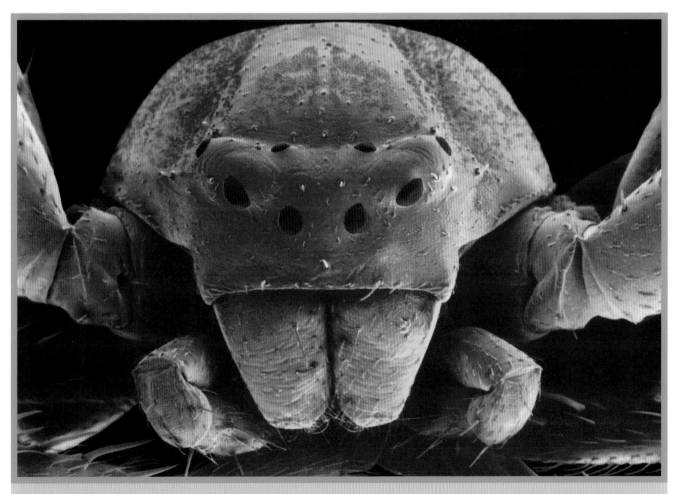

Crab spiders get their name from their ability to walk sideways, backward and forward. The specimen in this EM image is also known as the goldenrod spider because its abdomen can gradually change to the color of the goldenrod flower upon which it sits. It captures flies and bees two to three times its size. (x50)

Spitting Spider

All spiders suck in their food, but only a few kinds catch it with spit! There are seven known species of spitting spiders, which have the ability to spray sticky spit from their fangs. The sticky stuff is a concoction of silk, glue and venom made by the spitting spider's huge venom- and glue-producing glands.

This EM of a spitting spider (*Scytodes thoracica*) shows its six eyes (blue) arranged in three pairs. Its enormous carapace is shaped like a dome, and contains enlarged venom glands and glue compartments. (x4.4)

High-speed video has captured spit ejected from a spitting spider's fangs traveling at thirty meters per second—that's sixty-seven miles per hour, which is over the speed limit on most highways. The burst of spit lasts for about thirty milliseconds—the same amount of time as the blink of an eye.

While spitting, the spider rapidly moves its small chelicerae and fangs. This results in the release of zigzagging threads that look like a pattern of Silly String spray. The instant the spit hits the victim it contracts, tightening around the prey like shrink-wrap.

A hunter, the spitting spider doesn't spin webs. Yet, out of all the spiders on Earth, its spinnerets spin the toughest, strongest silk.

Why? Nobody knows.

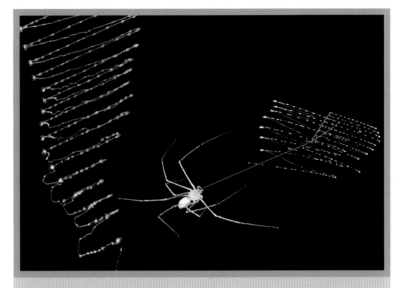

These zigzag spit patterns made by a spitting spider (*Scytodes thoracica*) were collected on a microscope slide. The left fang of one spider produced the enlarged pattern shown on the left. The straight line connecting the spider to the overlapping spit patterns on the right is typical of what would be seen for a brief moment after spitting, but in this case was added in Photoshop.

Spiny-Backed Orb-Weaver

Orb web-weaving spiders have seven or eight silk-making glands, more than any other kind of spider. They make the most elaborate webs, which are suspended by silk "cables" called frame lines and are attached to anchors, such as plants, walls or rocks. Of the seven different kinds of silk, frame lines are the strongest, able to hold up the entire web, the resident spider, its mate, its prey and often its offspring. It must also withstand wind and rain. A slight breeze tugging on a web would be similar to earthquake and hurricane forces hitting a suspension bridge or a skyscraper. The same super-strong silk that anchors a web is also used for draglines (recall the jumping spider and the spitting spider) and the gossamer kite strings of the baby balloonists.

The spiny-backed orb-weaver (*Microthena gracilis*) builds a web 20 feet above the ground, spanning wide gaps. The spines (red) on its tough abdomen make it less attractive to birds and other predators. (x4.8)

EM showing the spiny-backed spider's silk-gland spigots (yellow) and silk secretion (purple). (x2,695)

In addition to the super-strong dragline and frame-line silk, orb-weavers make several other types of silk. There is non-sticky capture silk. It is so stretchy that a large speeding insect such as a bee can crash into the web without damaging it. Long spiral silk provides a temporary frame on which the capture spirals are built. Attachment cement silk is used to hold the threads in place. Another kind of sticky silk coats the web for trapping prey. There is also tough waterproof silk for making egg cases and soft silk to line egg sacs.

The orb web is the picture that pops into people's heads when they think "spiderweb." The orb-weaver relies only on its sense of touch to build a new web every morning or night, depending on the species. The web takes about an hour to build, and is often eaten after it's been used.

Young spiders build messy-looking webs. Scientists think that the brain and body of a spider must be full-grown before the spider is capable of building a "perfect" web.

A golden orb-weaver in her web.

Many diurnal (daytime) spiders weave decorations into their webs. Zigzags, spirals and cross-shaped patterns may attract prey, defend against predators, provide camouflage or convey messages to people and pigs (oops, that's only in fiction).

Charlotte, the spider in E. B. White's classic children's book *Charlotte's Web*, was an orb-weaving barn spider. When Wilbur the pig first met her, he thought she was cruel and bloodthirsty. But as he got to know her, he realized she was kind and beautiful.

When Wilbur asked Charlotte why she wove the word "TERRIFIC" and other nice words into her webs, she replied:

"You have been my friend. That in itself is a tremendous thing. I wove my webs for you because I liked you."

Yes, spiders can be our friends!

This spiny-backed orb-weaver was photographed in its web in Congaree National Park, South Carolina.

This photo of the wasp spider (*Argiope bruennichi*) shows off its wasp-like pattern, which helps protect it against predators. It is a native of the Mediterranean region, and usually builds its web close to the ground in order to catch grasshoppers and crickets. The female measures about 18 mm in length.

In the Wild

Spiders often live nearby: in the garden, on a window, behind the couch, atop a lampshade, above the tub, under the bed. You could be within a few feet of a spider at this moment. Look and you may find one.

But wait! Resist the urge to squash a spider. What are you afraid of, anyway? Are you really in danger? You are a million times bigger than the average spider, and most spiders aren't poisonous to humans. Some suspected spider bites turn out to be infections caused by bacteria!

This photograph shows the dorsal, or top, view of a brown recluse spider (*Loxosceles reclusa*). Its bite is highly venomous.

If you live in the western United States, learn to identify the poisonous brown recluse by the violin-shaped mark on its prosoma, its dark legs and its six eyes (see eye pattern on page 12).

The recluse is a recluse, hiding in closets, behind furniture and under towels, so look before you reach. Although a bite from a brown recluse can cause a painful wound, it is rarely deadly—there are six recorded deaths from recluse bites, all before 1977. (However, always see a doctor if signs of illness or infection occur after being bitten by any spider.)

Friend a spider by taking its photo or recording it while it moves, spins a web, catches an insect, hatches or balloons away. Try to identify your friend. You may need to consult a spider expert, because identification can be tricky.

The Name Game

How do scientists identify spiders? Looking closely at different parts of the spider with the help of a microscope offers clues. Scientist Dennis Kunkel created each electron micrograph (EM) using a scanning electron microscope (SEM), a machine that "zooms in" and makes a digital picture. Before Dennis makes a picture he dries the specimen, mounts it on a stub and coats it with particles of gold. The SEM doesn't shine ordinary white light on the spider, so colors are not detected. Instead, it focuses another form of high energy, called electrons. An electron beam is used to make a picture of the spider. The result is a black-and-white image on a screen. A computer program (such as Photoshop) is used to color the picture. These are not the "real" colors of the spider, but are chosen by Dennis to show specific parts and details.

Some of the spiders in this book were collected by kids. A couple of hairy spiders came from a horse barn in Colorado. Dennis made an image of one of them, and we named it Devon's Spider after the girl who found it.

The digital photograph of sac spider specimens before Dennis made the SEM images shows the dorsal (top side) view on the left and the ventral (underside) view on the right.

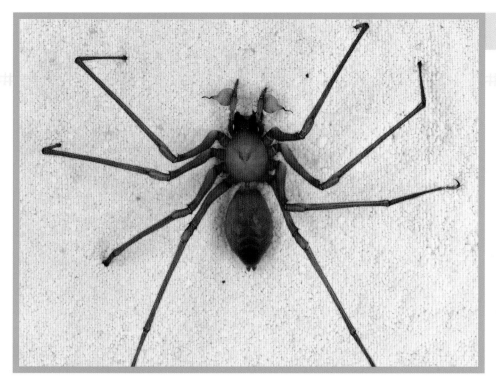

A cave robber spider.

To identify the spider we e-mailed a few black-and-white SEM images of the spider's parts to a spider scientist. Soon after, scientists throughout the world were looking at Devon's Spider. E-mails zipped back and forth: to Colorado, to New York City, to North Carolina, to Washington State, to Australia and to California. One scientist wanted to see an ordinary photograph of Devon's Spider. Luckily, Dennis had taken a regular photo with his digital camera. Using all the information available—the SEM images, the photograph, the size of the spider and the location where it was found—Devon's Spider was identified as a male sac spider (*Anyphaena dixiana*). A walking "pesticide," it eats crop-destroying insects and their eggs. When it isn't wandering around hunting down pests, it retreats to its silk sac under leaves, rocks or bark. To see Devon's Spider go to author Alexandra Siy's website (www.alexandrasiy.com).

What happens if a spider can't be identified? This happened when citizen scientists (like you) found an amazing-looking spider in an Oregon cave. It had big front claws and four staring eyes. In 2012, scientists decided that the strange spider was so different that it could only belong to a brand-new family of spiders. Named Trogloraptoridae, Latin for "cave robber," it is the first new spider family discovered in North America since the 1870s.

New spider species are discovered often. Perhaps there's a spider near you that will be one of them!

Eye Patterns

Eye patterns are sometimes used to identify spider families. These images show some distinct eye patterns of eight types of spiders.

Brown recluse spider

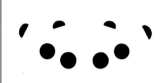

Diving bell spider

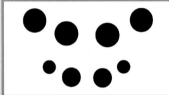

Fishing spider

Wolf spider

Black widow spider

Sac spider

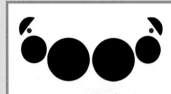

Jumping spider

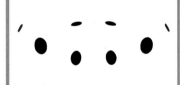

Crab spider

Spitting spider

Spiny-backed orb-weaver spider

How to Identify a Spider

Identification keys are used to identify animals and plants. Here's how it works: You answer simple questions about how the organism looks, and depending on the answer, the key tells you which question to answer next.

Here is a simple key to eight common arachnid orders. In the classification system, orders are groups that all belong to the same class—in this case the class is Arachnida, animals with four pairs of jointed legs.

SIMPLE KEY TO EIGHT COMMON ARACHNID ORDERS:

There are eight (four pairs) of jointed walking legs.

1.a. There is a tail .... go to 2

1.b. There is no tail .... go to 3

2.a. The tail is slender and needle-like .... it is a whip scorpion

2.b. The tail is broad and has a stinger .... it is a scorpion

3.a. There are a pair of scorpion-like claws .... go to 4

3.b. There are no scorpion-like claws .... go to 5

4.a. It is less than 5 mm (¼") long and flattened from top to bottom.......... it is a pseudoscorpion

4.b. It is 8 to 50 mm (1/3" to 2") long .... it is another type of whip scorpion

5.a. There appear to be one body part and no "waist" .... go to 6

5.b. There appear to be two body parts and a distinct "waist" .... go to 7

6.a. Legs are very long and slender compared to the body .... it is a harvestman (sometimes called daddy longlegs)

6.b. Legs are short compared to the body .... it is a mite or tick

7.a. First pair of legs is much longer than the rest .... it is a camel spider

7.b. First pair of legs is not much longer than the rest .... it is a true spider

How Spiders Fit into the Animal Classification System

Spiders belong to the **Kingdom Animalia**, which includes forms of life that have more than one cell and cannot make their own food like plants do. Humans, whales, worms, insects and birds are all animals.

Spiders also belong to the **Phylum Arthropoda**, which includes animals that have an exoskeleton and limbs with joints. Insects, crabs and lobsters are all arthropods.

Spiders also belong to the **Class Arachnida**, which includes arthropods that have four pairs of jointed legs. Scorpions, harvestmen, mites and ticks are all also arachnids.

Spiders then belong to the **Order Araneae**, which only includes arachnids that have spinnerets.

Mygalomorphae are a subgroup of Araneae that includes "primitive" spiders. These spiders have fangs that point directly down, and they cannot move their jaws from side to side. Tarantulas, trapdoor spiders and funnel-web spiders are all **mygalomorths**.

Arnaneomorphae are a subgroup that includes all "modern" spiders. These spiders have fangs that face one another and can pinch their prey and pick it up with movable jaws. Most spiders are **Araneomorphs**.

The subgroups are all divided into **Families**. There are more than 114 spider families.

Spiders are identified by their scientific names, which are always in Latin and consist of two words—the genus and species. For example, the scientific name of the cave robber spider is *Trogloraptor marchingtoni*. The species is named after the citizen scientist Neil Marchington, who discovered the spider. *Trogloraptor* (the genus name) means "cave robber," and was inspired by the spider's claws.

On the Web

The orb-weaver builds a new web every day. Websites on the Internet come and go, too, but here are some links to find more information, videos and images about spiders.

Governor Christie Saves School Children From Spider
A short, funny video showing the governor killing a spider
https://www.youtube.com/watch?v=bwjke6iRD14

Spider Myths (Burke Museum)
Myths, Misconceptions, and Superstitions About Spiders
http://www.burkemuseum.org/spidermyth/index.html

Identification of a Brown Recluse
http://spiders.ucr.edu/recluseid.html

Goliath Birdeater Tarantula
Video of one of the world's biggest spiders eating a mouse
http://video.nationalgeographic.com/video/tarantula_goliath

Spider Photos
http://kids.nationalgeographic.com/kids/photos/gallery/spider-webs/

The World Spider Catalog
Hosted by the American Museum of Natural History
http://research.amnh.org/iz/spiders/catalog/INTRO1.html

How Spiders See
Description of spider vision
http://australianmuseum.net.au/How-spiders-see-the-world

BIO Kids: Kids' Inquiry of Diverse Species
Information about many kinds of spiders
http://www.biokids.umich.edu/critters/Araneae/

A yellow garden spider.

More to Explore

Bishop, Nic. *Spiders*. New York: Scholastic, 2007.

Johnson, Jinny. *Simon & Schuster Children's Guide to Insects and Spiders*. New York: Simon & Schuster, 1997.

Levi, Herbert W., and Lorna R. Levi. *Spiders and Their Kin* (Golden Guide). New York: St. Martin's Press, 2002.

White, E. B. *Charlotte's Web*. New York: Harper, 1952.

Glossary

amber A hard, see-through yellow-, orange-, brown- or red-colored fossilized material. It is formed from the resin or pitch of ancient cone-bearing trees.

antivenom (also referred to as antivenin) A medicine that counteracts the toxic effects of harmful substances delivered by the bite of a poisonous animal such as a spider or snake.

arachnid A group in the animal classification system of arthropod animals. They are known as a class. Arachnids have four pairs of jointed legs, and include spiders, scorpions, ticks, mites, pseudoscorpions and harvestmen.

arachnophobia The fear of arachnids, usually spiders.

Arnaneomorphae In the animal classification system, the largest and most advanced subgroup of spiders. It is also called "modern" or "true" spiders.

arthropod An animal belonging to the largest group of animals (Arthropoda) called a phylum in the animal classification system. Members have legs with joints, many pairs of limbs and a hard outer skeleton (or exoskeleton). Insects, lobsters and centipedes as well as spiders belong to this phylum.

book lungs Breathing organs that bring air into contact with blood-filled layers. They look like tiny squares on the underside of the spider's abdomen.

carapace The hard covering of the front part (or prosoma) of a spider's body.

carnivore An animal that feeds on other animals.

chelicerae The mouthparts of a spider. They occur in pairs and are found in the front of the head beneath the eyes. The fangs are located at the ends of the chelicerae.

citizen scientists Ordinary people lacking specialized training in science, but involved in scientific research and discovery.

copper A reddish-colored metal. It is present in the blood of insects and spiders.

diurnal Active in the daytime.

dragline A silk safety thread that some spiders attach to rocks, plants or other stable objects.

egg Female sex cell that develops into a new organism if it is fertilized by a sperm cell from a male.

electron microscope An instrument used to create magnified images of scientific specimens. Images in the microscope appear as black-and-white because light is not used in the process.

exoskeleton The tough, waterproof outer covering of all arthropods, including spiders.

A black-and-yellow garden spider.

family A unit in the classification system consisting of related groups. There are 114 families in the order Araneae (spiders).

fang The sharp part at the end of each chelicera (or mouthpart) that a spider uses to inject venom into prey.

flexitarian A person or other animal whose diet is mostly vegetarian but occasionally eats fish, poultry or other kinds of meat.

fossil The remains or imprint of an ancient organism preserved in a petrified form, or as rock mold.

gland An organ in an animal that releases essential substances, such as proteins, into the body or into the animal's surroundings.

gossamer Long lines of silk used by spiders during ballooning. When abundant, gossamer can form a light film or sheet of silk.

harvestman An arachnid that lacks venom and has a pill-shaped, one-part body. (True spiders have two-part bodies.)

iron A hard, magnetic, silver-gray metal. It is present in some animal molecules, such as in human blood.

lateral Side part or view of something.

mate The act of female and male animals coming together during breeding.

membrane A thin, flexible sheet-like material that acts like a boundary or lining in a living organism.

mite A type of arachnid that is tiny. Many kinds live in the soil or on plants and animals.

molt The process of shedding the outer covering, or exoskeleton. This allows an animal to grow larger. Spiders molt between five and ten times, depending on the kind.

Mygalomorph One of the three divisions of spiders, also known as "primitive."

nocturnal Active during the night.

oxygen The colorless, odorless gas present in the air that supports life.

palps (also called **pedipalps**) The two leg-like feelers located in the front of the spider between the first pair of legs and the chelicerae.

paralyze To cause an animal or body part to no longer be able to move.

pheromone A chemical released from an animal that attracts or affects the behavior of another animal of the same species.

posterior The back, rear or hind end.

prosoma The front part of a spider's body (also called the cephalothorax).

protein Types of compounds found in all living things, especially in the parts that give support, strength and protection, such as silk, muscle and hair.

receptor A structure that detects a change in the environment, such as heat, light, movement or sound.

SEM The abbreviation for "scanning electron microscope," an instrument that makes greatly magnified images of scientific specimens.

setae Hair-like structures that may be shaped like bristles, feathers, hairs or scales. They usually detect vibrations.

silk A continuous natural fiber consisting of protein.

species A group of highly related organisms that mate and produce offspring.

sperm The sex cell produced by males that combines with the female's egg to produce a new organism.

spigot The tiny tube-shaped nozzle at the tip of the spinneret through which silk is released.

spinneret The cone-shaped organs located at the back end of a spider's abdomen that are connected to the silk-producing glands inside the spider.

sternum The oval-shaped plate of armor on the front and underside part of the spider.

tick The largest of the mites (which are arachnids). All ticks are parasites and attach their mouthparts to other animals to feed on blood.

venom Poisonous liquid made by animals that contain toxic compounds.

vibrate To move to and fro or from side to side.

Sources

BOOKS

Brunetta, Leslie, and Catherine L. Craig. *Spider Silk: Evolution and 400 Million Years of Spinning, Waiting, Snagging, and Mating*. New Haven, CT: Yale University Press, 2010.

Foelix, Rainer F. *Biology of Spiders*. 3rd ed. New York: Oxford University Press, 2011.

Herberstein, Marie Elisabeth, ed. *Spider Behaviour: Flexibility and Versatility*. United Kingdom: Cambridge University Press, 2011.

Hillyard, Paul. *The Private Life of Spiders*. Princeton, NJ: Princeton University Press, 2007.

Kelly, Lynne. *Spiders: Learning to Love Them*. Crows Nest, Australia: Jacana Books, 2009.

Michalski, Katarzyna, and Sergiusz Michalski. *Spider*. London: Reaktion Books, 2010.

Sims, Michael. *The Story of* Charlotte's Web. New York: Walker & Company, 2011.

Ubick, Darrell, Pierre Paquin, Paula E. Cushing, and Vince Roth, eds. *Spiders of North America: An Identification Manual*. Keen, NH: American Arachnological Society, 2005.

WEBSITES

Austin, A. D. "Life History of *Clubiona robusta* L. Koch and Related Species (Araneae, Clubionidae) in South Australia." *Journal of Arachnology* 12 (1984):87–104. http://www.americanarachnology.org/joa_free/joa_v12_n1/arac_12_1_0087.pdf.

Griswold, Charles, Tracy Audisio, and Joel Ledford. "An Extraordinary New Family of Spiders from Caves in the Pacific Northwest (Araneae, Trogloraptoridae, New Family)." *ZooKeys* 215 (2012): 77–102. http://www.pensoft.net/journals/zookeys/article/3547/an-extraordinary-new-family-of-spiders-from-caves-in-the-pacific-northwest-araneae-trogloraptoridae-new-family.

Hu, Xing Ping, Faith M. Oi, and Thomas G. Shelton. *The Black Widow*. Alabama Cooperative Extension System, 2002. http://www.aces.edu/pubs/docs/A/ANR-1039/ANR-1039.pdf.

Nagata, Takashi, Mitsumasa Koyanagi, Hisao Tsukamoto, Shinjiro Saeki, Kunio Isono, Yoshinori Shichida, Fumio Tokunaga, Michiyo Kinoshita, Kentaro Arikawa, and Akihisa Terakita. "Depth Perception from Image Defocus in a Jumping Spider." *Science* 335, no. 6067 (January 27, 2012): 469–471. https://www.sciencemag.org/content/335/6067/469.

A black-and-yellow garden spider.

Suter, Robert B., Patricia R. Miller, and Gail E. Stratton. "Egg Capsule Architecture and Siting in a Leaf-Curling Sac Spider, *Clubiona riparia* (Araneae: Clubionidae)." *Journal of Arachnology* 39 (2011): 76–83. http://www.americanarachnology.org/JoA_free/JoA_v39_n1/arac-39-01-76.pdf.

TED Institute. "Cheryl Hayashi: The Magnificence of Spider Silk," on *TED Talks*. TED Institute, 2010. http://www.ted.com/talks/cheryl_hayashi_the_magnificence_of_spider_silk.

U.S. Fish and Wildlife Service. *Kauai Cave Wolf Spider and Kauai Cave Amphipod.* U.S. Fish and Wildlife Service, 2010. http://www.fws.gov/pacificislands/Publications/Kauai%20Cave%20species%20fact%20sheet.pdf.

Image Credits

Center for Disease Control: 7
Center for Disease Control/Andrew J. Brooks: 39
Center for Disease Control/James Gathany: 10 (bottom)
Green, David I. (reproduced with kind permission from Siri Scientific Press): 13
Hetz, Stefan K.: 17
National Park Service: 36, 37, 44, 46, 47
National Park Service/Neal Herbert 2, 10 (top)
Schimming, Lynette: 12, 43
Siy, Alexandra: 21
Suter, PhD, Robert B.: 1, 33
U.S. Fish and Wildlife Service/Gordon Smith: 11
U.S. Fish and Wildlife Service/Mark A. Musselman: 19 (top), 23 (top)
U.S. Fish and Wildlife Service/Steve Hillebrand: 3
Wikimedia/George Chernilevsky: 14 (top)
Wikimedia/Masaki Ikeda: 38
Wikimedia/Quartl: 4
Wikimedia/Ryan Kaldari: 28 (bottom left)

Index

Golden silk orb-weaver.